beyond rock bottom

KARA PETROVIC

ISBN: 9781549530432

DEDICATION

Thank you to my cherry blossom, a tiger lily, a dandelion and my mother. Without you, this would not have happened. Thank you to JT, for giving me the idea in the first place. Thank you to my sister, who always did her best to point out the roads I had to take. Thank you to the friends who have stood by me as I shook and trembled, who gave me the courage to find my own strength, and who loved me though I gave no cause. And to you, dear reader, for sharing in my journey.

CONTENTS

A PREFACE

This is a collection of my writings that concern my illness, my trauma and reflect a negative time in my life. Yet still, I believe that this world can be filled with magic if you let it. I believe anything is possible, and that we all have some purpose, something valuable to contribute to the world — so long as we can find it within ourselves. I believe that people are kind at their core, and it's the world that makes them hard. I believe that deep down we know who the right people are. It's a feeling you can't describe or place, but you just know — they're the ones who matter, who will show up every time, who will be tied to you in this life. I believe we all have a light within us, and some of us either don't believe we're capable or we grew used to hiding it behind layers. There is no happy ending yet, but I'm alive, and that to me is good enough.

That being said: this collection contains poems that may be triggering for some, regarding topics of suicide, mental illness and sexual assault. Kindly now, dear reader.

PART ONE: FOR THE ONES WHO DID NOT LOVE ME

1.

ON SKEWED VIEWS

if you close your eyes

falling feels like flying

it's all a matter of perspective

like, to me—you were the sea

kissing the shore

and, to you—i was the sand

stuck in your shoe

though if i wait long enough

soon, you will be washed away too

trouble is

i will never be the tide to you.

in a way

i suppose it is only fair

—the universe entering into balance—

that i should know

what it feels like

to be on the other side.

you have put me through

a tropical storm

and i have put you through

barely an ocean breeze.

i realize now

while i am the person in flux

you are a steadfast stone

—unchanging and unmoving—

and as i research the art of forgetting

for you it has always been

as simple as turning away

so when i flew (fell)

you stood in place,

oblivious entirely

> —   *sometimes a shooting star is*
> *nothing but a speck of dust.*

2.

ON NAMES AND OTHER GAMES

if i were to ask you

what you knew of me

would you even know my name?

in recent months

i've come to think of my name

as a secret

rather, a gift

a treasure

one i must not give away

so easily

there is some culture

that believes

a name is power

and that by giving one's name

you are giving a part of yourself

and so i thought

if my heart is so easily won

perhaps it is better to save my name

at least it is the one thing

i can control

3.

ON NEEDLES AND YARN

to be deceived is to be

unwillingly tricked by another

but all you did was hand me the needle and
yarn,

and as i made my way up your body

my eyes glossed over any angry mark,

replaced it instead through pretty crochet,

into something i much preferred to see

your stony bones

became something soft to hold,

your bloodied hands

now pillowed from impact

but in the end i duped myself.

i have always been

a self-made fool.

see i was never suited

for domesticity.

i burn all i cook,

and stain my clothes pink

so when time came to be

all you had to do

was pull a stray thread

and leave me staring

at nothing but   empty space

4.

ON OPPOSITES

i think it was doomed right from the start

because, it was winter and:

i was sad but pretending to be happy

i wanted to be alone but i ended up with company

i hated being looked at but i still showed my body

i hated being touched but i let myself forget

it was winter but the weather was hot and humid

we were in a world where only opposites were true

and so it makes sense that 'see you later'

really meant

'i'll never talk to you'

5.

ON REFUNDS

every night i prayed

for a chance to peer inside your mind

i wanted nothing more

than to step right in

and search

for the corners or walls where my name was
etched

i wondered sleeplessly what it would look
like—

would it be red, or green, or perhaps (i
hoped) a deep shade of blue?

did the weight of it float around, or was it
dark, and heavy, and burdening?

i ordered a book online

one that had been titled

'thoughts of me'

and written by you

i paced by my door and wrung my hands,

ever impatient, ever waiting to understand

in my mind I painted its image,

daydreaming about whether it would
compare to mine,

whether they would be mirrors to one another
in their own right,

mine:

where dozens of pages were filled

with just your name,

carved so fiercely near the end   that it cut
through the paper,

that you could hardly understand

what it was   you were trying   to read

i paced by the door, and when it arrived, i
wasted no time—

i, who is usually so delicate

so careful

so hesitant—

in opening it up, only to find:

a cover

a back

and a single

blank

page

6.

ON FOOLISH DREAMS

listen.

it wouldn't have hurt so much if she wasn't
the girl i always wanted to be.

in high school i carved the word ugly into my
skin

so that even if i once reached

that pivotal point of high self esteem

i would always be reminded of who i was

underneath it all

and i wanted so badly to be

the athletic girl

who put makeup on effortlessly

who knew a thing or two about fashion

whose laughter sounded like flowers
blooming

who knew what it meant to be sad,

and anxious,

but in the beautiful way

in the mysterious way

in the way that could be cured by true love's
kiss

whose skin was always soft

and hair always brushed

—sometimes styled—

long, and long, and dark, and wavy

a fine contrast against her light eyes

and pale skin

that never led anyone to question

just where she was from

whose body hair was fine,

or at least taken care of

so frequently and expertly,

that no one ever questioned

just where she fell in human evolution

whose body curved in all the right places

whose skin was taut with muscle

and soft and inviting where it should be

who ate right

who never smoked

and never tried to end her life;

once, twice, seventeen times

who liked art but didn't really understand it

who studied hard even though she hated it

who cared about injustice but not to the point

that too much thought would lead her to

unending, selfish tears

whose eyes could stop an army

and whose lips never fell into a thin line

whose kisses you remember

and whose body you miss

when you're lying in a bed without her

whose warmth you reach out

for not just from habit or desire

but need—desperate need

who didn't make loving her hard

who you missed,

even when you were with another

the girl who everyone knew was beautiful—

they just knew, ok. they just knew her name

and they would say:

'yes, her. she's very beautiful.'

i longed for proverbial flowers

to be thrown at my feet

to wear pink,

and heels,

and dresses,

and not feel like ripping my skin off

because of it.

i longed to not be afraid

when men stare at me for too long,

because i knew i was worth staring at,

because i knew they could hurt my heart

but i never learned how they could destroy
my body

it wouldn't hurt so much if you weren't

everything i was looking for,

everything i wanted,

and so was she

7.

ON DEFINITIONS

A BULLET, A BLADE, A BOY

definition:

a projectile for firing from a rifle,
revolver, or other small firearm,
typically made of metal, cylindrical
and pointed, and sometimes
containing an explosive,

the part of a sharp weapon, tool, etc,
that
forms the cutting edge,

a male child or young man.

used in a sentence:

> to be bludgeoned belligerently, to
> bleed in betrayal, to be left for dead
> by a bullet, a blade, and a boy
> who was only ever in it
> for the kill

8.

ON THE PRECIPICE

it's just—

i know i am a weak person

and i know it's my fault

for getting all wrapped up

and sometimes i wonder.

(and by sometimes

i mean all the time,

because the number of times i've
thought of you in the last hour

is infinite,

and even still the number of times i
haven't

i've been thinking about how stupid i
am,

how angry i am with myself for
getting so caught up

for letting my illness idealize

yet another person

who would only enjoy

hurting me)

do i love you? do i even care?

or is it just that you made me laugh

in a way i didn't think was possible anymore

and i haven't felt a damn thing for anyone in
a really long time?

(am i so hungry for happiness and so

desperate to feel love

that i'm crushed to realize

just at the precipice

not only was it not to be —

but it wasn't what i thought, at all?)

i wanted,

i wished,

i wanted,

i wished

(but wishes and wants

are meant to be spent on the stars.

not people whose faces

rival that of a hexagonal die,

whose hearts change direction

like the earth rotates around the sun,

around itself,

misshapen and tilted,

as trusted as it is not to be trusted.

a heart is not weighted by gravity,

but tied by arteries

and each time it opens and closes,

it changes its mind)

look.

i know fairytales aren't real.

(somewhere, deep down, i suppose,

i know that the prince

doesn't rescue the princess,

that the underdog doesn't get the girl,

that the beat-up team

never wins the playoffs,

that summer lovin' happens fast

for a reason

and people like me

don't end up with guys like you)

and you'd think by now

i'd have learned my lesson.

but here i am again

looking at all the parts of me

that have decided against my will

to make you everything

so that the only way i can move on,

the only way i can make you mean nothing,

is to carve myself empty

9.

ON MY MOUNTAIN HOME

i stood outside your door with an open palm

and a smile on my face

i said, look i found your favourite flowers

one and three were clenched together tightly
in my hands

i was vibrating at a frequency you couldn't
understand

but you always said you'd love me

so i thought you wouldn't mind

if i visited you from the highest of mountains

instead the corner of your lips turned down

and your brows were furrowed

you ask me:

when was the last time i slept? the last i
showered? or ate?

    slept? showered? ate?

        showered? ate? slept?

           ate? slept? showered?

and when i said i didn't know

you told me i shouldn't come around here
anymore,

that you couldn't listen anymore,

that i had said the same thing

six times in a row

and now i was shouting

and the neighbours can hear

and you don't like the way they look at us

when we're together

i thought you would like me like this

i thought we could

take over the world like this

with me, buzzing and optimistic

instead of trapped within a dark room

and shying away from any light

i thought you would like me like this

like this

    like this

       like this

but you're shutting the door

and you won't let me say goodbye

i loved you so much i would have done
anything you asked,

so when you asked me to dive into the ocean

i did,

even though i was afraid

but when i asked for you to come with me

you said you wouldn't dream of it

    you wouldn't dream of it

        you said you wouldn't dream of it

you told me i had a winter heart

that i was cold

and all i would ever be was ice, ice, ice

you said the only thing i was good for

was giving people grief

you took me apart

and pieced me back together

the way you liked best

i told you the parts didn't fit right,

weren't put together properly

but you smiled and said you knew best

and i,

i loved you so much,

i would have done anything you said

10.

ON THORNS

there is a thorn stuck in my leg.

i ask you once then twice if you feel it,

you tell me i've asked you this before

i sew my lips into a smile and you tell me

it's the prettiest i've ever been

there is a thorn stuck in my leg.

i tell you i'm itching, itching,

the kind of itch i can't escape from,

the kind of itch that has no start,

no end,

and no middle at all.

the kind of itch that makes me want to rip my

skin off

and you say i'm talking too much

so i turn the volume down on my brain

and you thank me for the quiet

there is a thorn stuck in my leg

or my arm

or my neck

it's the same, i say

it's the same

even if it isn't

there is a thorn stuck in my leg

and i am buzzing, buzzing, buzzing

until you ask if maybe i am the bee

and i am the one who has stung herself

you laugh but i think you're afraid

there is a thorn stuck in my leg—

i am smiling

a thorn—

i am screaming

a thorn—

i am smiling

a thorn—

there is a thorn stuck in my leg

i'm laughing now

you say it sounds like i'm crying

and you wish i would stop

so i reach in with jagged hands

and pull out my lungs

laying them out like lovely flowers,

laying them out like the reddest of roses,

laying them out like only you could have
seen,

and you tell me,

you tell me,

it's the prettiest i've ever been

11.

ON SMOKE

i think i really did love you in a way i never
had before.

i think love always shows up in different
ways,

and no new love is the same as the last.

and while i am a cynic at heart,

i do believe in love,

at least for just a short little while:

the all-encompassing feeling,

the desire to walk step in step with another
person,

and the swelling of your chest when they
walk in a room.

i've heard tales from older women

who say they still feel that excitement,

even after forty years.

well for me, i had only lived that twice,

and both times just as long as the last,

or shorter,

or longer,

depending on how you decide to count the
time.

i am a half-piece,

a shadow,

and a shell,

but i know that i love wholly

and i love truly.

and the first person i loved nearly swallowed
me whole,

but you showed me what more life had to
offer.

to me, you were the sun,

and i was the moon,

reflecting your light.

to me you were all the answers,

even to questions i didn't know i was asking.

to me you were the good—

in the world,

in me.

to me you were comfort.

security.

stability.

and i always thought

it was because i was afraid

that i felt something so intrinsically wrong
  in my bones as time went on.

my soul was screaming at me to run

while everyone else i knew was chastising
me to stay.

but in the end my flight won out and i left.

and i told you to find your own love.

and you did.

but the truth came out,

like it always has,

and it always will,

my long lost false love

and in that instant

i learned all that i refused to see about you.

that you were just the same as the first,

that you were just as cruel as the last,

and just as manipulative as what i had
suffered.

and i guess i thought,

maybe once,

maybe this time,

i would be wrong.

that someway,

somehow,

in the future,

you'd shape up and fight

for what you insisted you wanted.

but i should have known.

because all you were was smoke and mirrors,

and i just got caught up in the fog

12.

ON REQUESTS

lovely lion,

with your claws twelve inches long,

won't you sink your teeth

into the back of my neck once more?

won't you parade me around,

march me to and fro,

showing me all there is to know,

and telling me i am your sweetest pet?

lovely hawk,

with your talons made of lonsdaleite,

won't you pluck me

from the earth once more?

won't you soar into the sky,

with me in your clutches,

at blinding speeds,

showing me all i deserve to see,

and telling me i am your only darling?

is this not love,

dear lion, dear hawk?

shall i forever wait,

in the savannah,

in the meadow,

where you tossed me aside,

longing to be picked up again?

13.

ON FORGETTING

days are split,

between when i feel

as though i am forged of iron,

indestructible and fierce

and days in which i feel

i am a dandelion sort of person,

designed to break apart

at the slightest gust of wind

on the day i was a flower,

waving to and fro

you found me,

and told me that a dandelion

grows through anything

grows despite everything

and when all is said and done

all it does is spread sunshine

i promised to remember that.

you were the wind,

but instead i was swept up in you

around you and through you

you reeked of poison,

but all i could smell were roses.

you watered me in the river Lethe,

and i could never have enough

when you left, without a final drop,

the echo of you grew,

surrounding me in smoke and dust

i try to shake your ghost

but it is embedded in my shadow

so that now i can no longer bloom

i had asked, with mirth in my tone,

is this the part where you eat my heart?

tear it out with your daggers for teeth,

and flaws for hands?

your gaze was cold

but you smiled

nonetheless

     —   *i am tired of dreaming of you.*

14.

ON REMEMBERANCE

i am not

that person

for a lot of people

i am nothing but

lingering smoke

and distorted mirrors

sometimes, on occasion,

the trick can last for a while

but it always fades

i become a photograph

a snapshot.

a memory of an imprint,

the name of which will fade after time.

maybe, one day,

each ship i have jumped

while still on shore

will leave my mind as well

it is selfish of me to wish i was

a lingering scent

for this venomous tongue

could never speak in love.

i am the one who has always pulled the plug

without the doctor's permission

each and every time

yet all at once i was enraptured by your
beauty,

endeavoured to receive your love

you were the song stuck in my head,

a record skipping a beat,

always on the tip of my tongue,

but never quite within reach.

with bloodied hands

i dug for the person within myself

who could be someone

you'd look at in light

if only i could just

fit into that mould

you might just see me

as someone worth seeing

as someone worth remembering

15.

ON THEORY

i often find myself falling for someone

who refuses to catch me,

and likewise upon waiting arms

i suddenly develop a fear of heights.

either i'm unlucky in love

or i'm obsessed with the theory

but not the practice.

maybe i shy away from jumping when i
know i'll be caught

because the excitement is gone,

or maybe i shy away because it means
committing.

commitment is only something i'm willing to do

when the reality leads to impossibility.

i digress.

your stupid smile is burned within my mind,

ice blue eyes always call to me but never answer.

i have this urge to destroy you with my touch,

to run my hands across your body and leave

the same fiery feeling

you've left

across mine

it is a very strange thing —

to want to be loved

when you do not know

how to be

it's been ages and yet still I'm longing

but i think i am destined to want

and never receive

<u>PART TWO: FOR WHEN LOVE WAS NOT ENOUGH</u>

1.

OF MYSELF

My whole life—

I have lived for others.

I have based my decisions on the happiness
of others.

I have led a life that ensures everyone is
pleased—everyone but me.

And it has left me emptied and without a
sense of who I am—

What I want, what I need, what I am looking
for and what will leave me happy.

But then—finally—I moved on

I began to live for myself.

And I am sorry, but I am not ready to give
that up.

Love is not fated.

There is not one great love waiting for you,

that was written for you long ago.

People were not made for people,

they were made with artisanal care,

a soft breath given to them by God,

sent out into the world to find their own way.

Love is not destiny.

Love is hard. Love is a choice. Love is compromise.

Love, above all, is work.

If you are asking me to choose—

Between my current dreams and the path I am heading down on

If you are asking me to choose—

Between finally becoming at peace with
myself and finding my place in the world

If you are asking me to choose—

Between my happiness and yours

Between my life and love

My choice is clear

And it is not you.

Maybe this is a mistake—but it is one I am
willing to make.

It is a loss I am willing to risk.

The truth is, I have never valued love as
much as I value my family,

my friends

and my joy.

This is not the fault of a childish mind.

This is not a fault at all.

This is me, this is a trait I have developed

and one I am content with.

But if you love me like you say you do,

you'll leave me be.

You'll let me live my life.

You'll let me choose my own happiness.

I hope that you, too, will find your peace.

Your place.

And someone who loves you,

the way you're never going to get from me.

2.

OF THE GRAND CANYON WITHIN

I once drew you a map

and pointed out the canyon

you created.

You marvelled at its grandness

and wondered how I led a life

split so in half.

In vain I explained

but your ears were filled

with too much dirt

to comprehend

any of my hurt.

Here is my garden,

filled from side to side

with rotting flowers

choked by endless weeds.

Remember once you called them charming

couldn't see how they were alarming

when compared to the unkept grass

which you decided was far too crass.

This is my home,

cased with ice glazed windows

and cracked right in the middle

kept frozen in a single moment.

Staring endlessly

at my little sea

of misshapen

memories.

My compass is flawed,

you told me this could never be ours,

and laughed when I told you

I navigate by stars.

You saw numbers

where I saw signs,

I was never quite able

to calibrate myself

by your designs.

You chose not to watch

as I picked through the shards,

those often mishandled with care.

Instead you asked if i had ever bled

within your precious stead.

Just over the horizon,

past the hills

and past the valleys,

I saw what you would not.

My routes were carved into the page,

as clear as a moonless night,

a cloudless day,

or an open stage.

'Here.' I would say,

'here lies my pain.'

But all you saw

was what we shared in vein.

I had begged you to stay,

I had asked you to change,

you are stuck in your way,

and I am doomed to be

always just out of the range.

You are the sunrise,

and I am the sunset,

you are the moon,

and I am a star.

'We are here,' you tell me,

'we are close.'

But we have never been

more far.

3.

OF ANSWERS

'You run away from feelings.'

'Yes,' I said.

'That wasn't a question'

'Yes,' I said. But for me it always was.

A question of yes or no,

of stay or leave,

of safety or pain.

I am unwell.

I wish to say it from the rooftops,

to scream into the woods,

to tell the world of my suffering.

It rests always at the tip of my tongue:

I am unwell,

I am unwell,

I am unwell.

4.

OF MY TRUTHS

I hear it buzzing

in the back of my mind

whispering dreams and other cruel things

of a world where I am free

From the demons resting   within me.

And you say,

'Dear,

why does it have to be this way?

Let me find what was lost,

let me fix what is gone.'

But

hush now,

your voice is too loud

and your soul too great

for my small hands to carry.

So let me shatter all my bones

as I seek to recreate

what long ago was burned from my skin.

I seek no sympathy

I ask for no salvation

simply to be left

to fall apart in peace

to fall apart in pieces

to fall apart in peace.

You desire my wellness

but I am too forgone

and I am too far gone.

You ask me to believe you

your heart so full of love

you say the world is ours to conquer.

But hush now

take back your protests.

They fall upon deaf ears

ones that will take and twist

and twist and take

until your words become nothing but hate.

So let me shatter all my bones

as I seek to recreate

what long ago was burned from my skin.

I am a lying heart,

with a wicked smile

I fool them all.

I take what is given

and make no efforts to return.

Your tears,

your cries,

Reach for a false name.

I seek no sympathy

I ask for no salvation

simply to be left

to fall apart in peace

to fall apart in pieces

to fall apart in peace.

I seek no sympathy

I ask for no salvation

Simply to be left

to fall apart in peace

to fall apart in pieces

to fall apart in peace.

Let me shatter all my bones

as I seek to recreate

what long ago was burned away.

5.

OF NUMBNESS

Sometimes I write the same words or phrases

over and over again,

until they no longer have any meaning.

They get stuck in my head on endless repeat,

and the stop button is broken,

or maybe it never existed at all.

So I take out my pen and I write it,

over and over and over again,

until it can no longer hurt me.

Until I am numb to the words,

and entirely numb to feeling.

But—

I want to feel again.

Not the way I do now,

the highs that take me out of this world,

and the lows that crash over me like a tidal wave.

The in-between of nothingness,

and the ever present paranoia.

I want to feel in the most purest of ways,

to smile for nothing,

to cry for something,

I want to feel again.

So that maybe,

I can love.

6.

OF CHOICES

I feel that I could be loved so greatly

and wholly

if I just let myself be loved.

It is right there at my fingertips

but I am still too afraid to touch.

I am endlessly fascinated

by tales of others' love—

a view into a world I can never be a part of.

For my love is fleeting

(as I make it so)

and it is something

I can never know firsthand.

It is beautiful,

it is sickening,

it is envious.

It is theirs.

But never mine.

I attach myself to ideas

rather than people.

Forever more enchanted

with the thought of someone

than the person themselves.

7.

OF CONTRADICTIONS

I would swap out my heart

for another if I could.

One that is not chained

by sorrow and misery,

one unafraid to love wholly.

I am a walking contradiction.

All at once,

I am loving, open, sensitive to heartbreak

yet—

callous, cruel, easily fleeing.

I am a person of misshapen parts,

skin sewed together,

only to be sheared apart.

my heart filled with jagged glass,

softness long since lost

and beating through stubborn will alone.

I want, I long,

I run, I hide away.

You must not see

the parts of me

that even I am too ashamed

to look at.

The parts of me that you love,

have been carefully constructed,

an outfit laid out and chosen,

all the wrinkles pressed.

I cannot love you,

because I cannot have you see me.

And what is love—

if not seeing clearly?

8.

OF HESITANCE

I have kissed many.

Men and women alike,

young and old,

strong and weak.

I have felt their lips

atop my own

and I have stood

still as a stone

as their hands traced a map

across my body.

I have let myself

be painted in their fingertips,

be moulded in their grip.

I have felt warm,

I have felt cold,

I have felt nothing at all.

But the ghost of your lips

of the kiss that never was

lingers on mine

with feelings much deeper

than ever I have felt.

And oh,

how I wish,

how I wish,

when you had asked

—by God, by God, you had been the first to

ask—

I had the courage

to say yes.

9.

OF THE VOID

And when I fell,

I fell from the atmosphere,

but the ground did not cushion my fall.

I plummeted deep within the earth,

just missing oblivion

but nestling instead

into the centre of the void.

I grew comfortable here

I let it seep into my bones.

And I can hear you calling

I can see you reaching

but alas I cannot feel

anything at all.

10.

OF THE FLOWERS

I sat and peeled the petals

of an old and withered rose

the poor thing weeped,

'I am already dying,' said she,

'why must you continue

to rip me at my seams?'

Relentless in my pursuit,

I persisted,

until there was nothing left

but a tired and old stem

bristling with thorns.

— *Oh, how I wanted to love you.*

PART THREE: FOR WHEN I DID NOT LOVE MYSELF

1.

LITTLE WISHES

i wish to wear shiny things,

to glow as i walk down the street

glittering even through the greyest of days

i wish to be as bright as the sun

so that when people look at me

they have to squint

just to see even a portion   of my brilliance

i wish to be a star

but instead i am a rock,

like anyone else

easily passed by.

i wish i was a doe,

with soft eyes

and a bright smile

with fragile skin

and a warm touch

but instead i am a shard,

that which is made of the coldest ice,

the sharpest thorns,

and the most impenetrable of metals

i wish i was the sun,

shining down on everyone,

brightening their day

but instead i am a storm,

wild, untamed, and destructive

raining down on everyone

and ruining their day

2.

LITTLE CHANGES

a wall has been built around you,

made of steel and covered in thorns

to help you pretend

pain is imaginary

and weakness is a call for help

you with your eyes like ice,

and cruel smile,

was once a child,

warm and hopeful

always seeking kindness

— *whatever happened to those gentle hands?*

3.

LITTLE QUESTIONS

how does it happen?

how does a child with love in their heart,

so wide and so large that it could consume
them,

but instead empowers them,

energizes them,

and teaches them that the world is their
oyster—

become an adult with shaky hands?

with shoulders collapsing

under the weight of thoughts

that once whispered promises of joy

but now exclaim only warnings of doom?

and do mothers look at me,

with my permanently embedded frown,

with my frightened expression

and weakened countenance,

and wonder:

how does this happen?

could this happen?

to my son,

who dreams of being a football player,

and who is always laughing

and running

and filled with so much energy

that it astounds me?

to my daughter,

who dreams of being a scientist,

and who is always reaching,

and always asking questions,

whose mind is so bright

i wonder how i could be so lucky?

or do they think:

why, this poor thing!

a victim of a poor mother no doubt!

not my children, not now, not ever!

because they don't know that my mother

was haunted by her own demons

and did nothing but her best

to be a steady figure of love and support,

of guidance and boundaries.

that my mother

is a woman forged from the iron of the gods,

that if I was a storm

my mother was the original hurricane that
created me,

that my mother held her head high,

even with ten twenty pound stones

tied around her neck,

that my mother loved me

in days when she did not love herself,

in days when my illness

had me calling her a demon,

a witch, or Satan himself.

that my mother is not the reason

i chose to let blood flow from my veins,

but that she is the reason

i am breathing still to this day,

that she would patiently pry my hands,

holding them down,

to prevent them from clawing at my skin,

that while i screamed and cried,

she cooed at me,

and held me,

and told me i would survive this,

i will always survive this

that my mother has made mistakes,

ones she cannot change,

ones she will carry in her heart,

and ones she has never stopped,

never ceased,

trying to undo

see my mother raised me

with a wolf in my chest,

and when i howl,

she is howling too,

and if i am a goddess,

my mother is the titan that came before me,

unfathomably powerful,

and the fabric of my very universe.

i wish i could say i don't know either.

i wish i could tell them i hear their thoughts

as if their eyes could speak,

and that they pierce through my skin

and add to my guilt,

that i was sorry

to take up so much space

and worry them,

that really i was trying my best

to be as small and quiet as possible.

i wish i could say i try to figure it out myself,

i try to discover where i went wrong,

and that if i could build a time machine

i would go back to that exact moment   and change

everything.

but i never learned quite how to speak—only placate

4.

LITTLE GARDENS

i have been cursed

with silence.

there is a garden growing

within my chest,

threatening to burst

with bruises on my hands

i beg myself to open

but I would rather bleed in silence

than cry in the open

i have a reserve in the corner of my mind

where my tears reside

and that is how I keep my soul alive

(you cannot be hurt if you keep yourself

locked up ,

but i somehow manage to water away)

i am suffocating from the inside out

i am tortured by my quiet needs and desires

and all at once i am seized

lightning has struck my vision

i am frozen in place

i am frozen to my core

memory, you cruel beast,

is no place safe from your reach?

i open my lips to speak

a thousand pennies fall out beneath

the world is too loud

this burden too heavy

for me to continue to carry

— *and so, i crumble within*

5.

LITTLE CLOUDS

when i open my eyes i see nothing

i forgot about these days

the solid stretches of emptiness

where time slips away from me

and i cannot write anything worthwhile

this is my favourite version of myself

the version that does not exist

i am grey within

and i am grey without

i sit indoors by the windowsill

and stare as the world passes me by

i am tipped at the precipice

of well and not

of sad and not

these are the stretches of the in-between

my inner self has checked themselves out

i am grey within

and i am grey without

i am inhabiting a shell

that has long since been left vacant

i have no refuge

no place to find my sanity

i am hollowed out

for i am grey within

and i am grey without

6.

LITTLE VOID

within my chest there rests a black hole

large and all consuming

most days i cannot breathe

when it is at its worst

and i find there is no refuge from my mind

i seek to find some sort of external way

to escape from this eternal void

so i drink six coffees a day.

i'm told tea

would be better for my health

but i find tea does not reach within me

and ignite my heartbeat

as i so desperately need.

i was once told my defining characteristic

was my yawn

i would have hoped it would have been my
charm

or my humour

but such things exist only in my mind.

i am an empty shell

we do not speak of the days of in-between

the stretches that rest

in the middle

of the mountains and the valleys

the thick grey fog that surrounds my mind

its wet air chills my bones

and i can feel them creaking each time i
stand.

they ask me where i have gone to

what place i visit within my mind

but there is nothing

only grey

7.

LITTLE GHOSTS

Lucifer, dear, i wish you would stop calling

i have changed my number,

my name,

my address,

yet somehow you manage to find me

again and again

your persistence is managing to wear my
resistance thin

like every man i've ever been with

i find myself slowly backed into saying yes

to your demands to join you in the afterlife

to your promises i will burn like i so dearly
believe i deserve

i exist only in your perception of me

you remind me all i am

is a shadow of a person,

perfectly form fitted

to what the situation calls for,

and an empty ghost   that ceases to exist

when i am alone

you swear it will be an eternity

you swear i will simultaneously be alight
with flame

and left in the darkness

Lucifer, i hear you calling

Lucifer, you know me so well

you know just what makes my body shiver
with joy

and anticipation

you tell me i am living in a purgatory,

a grey world where i am already dead

and it's high time

i make a decision

i am a liar, i am a sinner,

dealing in half-truths and stories,

i do not belong in the kingdom of heaven, i know

and i know now i do not even belong in the kingdom of earth

my one place is a citizen of yours

my one place is to resign to your call

and join you

once and for all

8.

LITTLE WOLVES

i am the opposite of the boy who cried wolf

i am the boy who went silently as the wolves
came around

i am the boy who allowed the wolf to maul
him alive

i am the boy who went down without even a
whisper

and left the pieces of himself out for
everyone to find

i am the boy who watched

detached and separate

as they were forced to sew him back together

i am not the boy who cried wolf

i welcome their teeth, i lay beneath them
bare—

i am numb to feeling;

i know no fear

i flirt with them, i toy with them, i mimic
their howls at the lonely moon

and when they come for me i am no longer
scared

but i forget i am attached to others

for when they sewed me back together,   they
did it with their own thread

with tiny strings they are connected to me

the slightest tug will send them running

colliding into me

alert at the smallest sign of danger

certain a fight has begun

certain it's one i'm willing to lose

because i am not the boy who cried wolf

i am the wolf

and they are all crying for me

9.

LITTLE LIES

they say you must lie to yourself

lie, they tell me, until you believe it

so here is a list of lies:

i have never worried a day in my life

i have never felt the feeling of a python

wrapping itself around my chest

stealing my breath pitilessly.

i have never shaken, vibrating with intensity,
at

sending a message

having a conversation

walking into a room of people

or staring at nothing at all.

i have never thought

i would be better off—

i have never gasped   ·

and lost my sight

i have never been taken back

to that one and horrible night

i have never thought

i would be better off—

i have never been sad, not for a single
second.

i have never woken up to find

somebody replaced the blood in my body

with cement

i have never struggled to lift myself

out of bed   to face the day

i have never thought

i would be better off—

i have never felt as if,

the most mundane of tasks,

were suddenly monsters i had to fight

except i had no weapons

i wore no armour

and i was weaker than i had ever been.

i have never thought

i would be better off—

i have never willed myself to cry

so that maybe

it might ease the pain

i have never felt like a failure

a burden

a waste of space

i have never felt

i would be better off—

i have never searched

for the smallest of signs

like the way my hands open and close

around the covers of my blanket

to convince myself to stay—

i have never played with the Morai,

toying with their scissors,

and daring them to make the cut

shouting to the Heavens,

just how much i wished

just how much i would be

could be

better off—　　*(alive, alive,*

　　　　　it is always alive,

　　　　　　with your hands

　　　　　　　and your touch

　　　　　you are someone's

　　　　never enough

　　　and never once

　always too much)

10.

LITTLE PROMISES

i have too many thoughts

and i've made a recent promise to myself

to stop talking so damn much,

to stop sharing all my thoughts,

as if they were

some profound philosophical revelation

in any case.

it is tiring for all parties involved,

the constant ups and downs,

the stretches of nothing in between

but i promise, i vow to you,

i am officially sick

of the sound of my own voice

and entirely unable

to withstand the emotional hangover

that comes afterwards.

i am well aware my illness,

disorder,

whatever, whatever,

is of my own doing.

that i can change it.

but it's also hard,

and terrifying,

to abandon my comfort blanket

and fall forth blindly

and yet simultaneously

actively work to rewire my brain

i don't mean

to be so pathetic

and depressing,

so helpless and constantly in crisis,

so obnoxiously selfish.

but i'm trying

i'm trying to change

and i wish i had that on a business card,

to spare myself the trouble

of sharing out loud

11.

LITTLE NOTES

1.i fear the dark.

    not literally, but the darkness resting
within me has made itself a home and is
moving to evict me from the premises

2.i am alone.

    except I am surrounded by people
constantly to the point where I am
exhausted and yet still disconnected

3.i am alive.

    but only by appearances, for all intents
and purposes I have long since been
dead
and remain a shadow amongst the living

12.

LITTLE LONG ISLAND

well, okay.

for example,

this drink,

this Long Island

—and before you ask, no,

i'm not supposed to be drinking while i'm on
my medication—

i'm drinking it,

and the thought pops into my head:

this is what i was drinking the night i was
raped.

i've had it since then,

it's not like I haven't,

and i've had good times on it.

but that's what i'm thinking about.

that's the thought that comes to mind.

and it's like, why am i like that?

why does my brain insist

on reminding me of worser times?

why do i choose to think of painful things?

even when i'm recovering,

my brain doesn't want to let me forget the things

i've had to swallow in the past.

and it ruins even the best of times

13.

LITTLE TRIGGERS

Triggered!—

a terrible word owned by terrible people!—

their smirk is carved in skin—

their self-righteousness blinding—

as a simple simple word

rips me limb from limb

i must grow a thicker skin

i must grow a thicker skin

i must grow a thicker skin

it is funny to witness—

as i am shaking, sobbing, scratching my
throat

is it, is it, is it?

i want to burn my eyes from my skull

i want to rip my tongue from its cavern

i want to claw through my very own skin

i want to tear myself limb from limb

funny, funny, funny,

i laugh along in jest,

i dare not speak against,

i am ashamed of my illness,

i wear no medal of honour

upon my chest

my scars not visible

for the world to see,

though my skin has become impenetrable

i too, share Achilles' heel,

i too, am brought down

by the simplest of things

my life in tatters

my life in tatters

my life in tatters

i must pack up the ends

i must sew myself together again

and I must apologize

for being so damn

Sensitive!

14.

LITTLE REALITIES

at 14 years old, sex was a mystery

it was a whispered giggle

passed around between bathroom stalls

that summer i learned

my virginity was not a thing to be lost

but taken

i learned that it is better to say yes

than have a 'no' be mistaken

and i learned what it meant

to fear being left alone with a man

who was not yet spent

in high school i was taught

that my body was a commodity

to be traded and bet upon

to be used and left abused

and laughed at as i walked down the halls

i began to separate:

a person on the streets

and dead inside in the sheets

when a man presents his piece

do as you're told

and get down on your knees

my worth is defined

by whether or not i've stayed in line

and god forbid

i say no

god forbid

i say don't, please

god forbid

i act like a tease

and i must apologize

for making you believe a lie

i must tilt back

smile

and delicately arch my back

and after you've cum as you please

i must thank you

for your effort

i know now

that i am just an empty vessel

for you to release your tension

and leave me behind

as you exchange high fives

with your friends

and mimic my expressions

and pride yourself on all the stops you pulled

to get me

to agree

to sleeping with you

as if i am not a person,

but a conquest,

mysterious foreign land

for you to conquer

and mark your territory

i am nothing but prey

a lamb to be slaughtered

it doesn't matter

if i wanted it or not

it doesn't matter if i was willing

no matter how i hide

and how i fight

they will find me

they will take me

and in the end

they will leave me

15.

LITTLE PERSON

you will create this idea, this notion

that if you can just make yourself

as small as possible

as hidden as possible

they won't see you

and there

they can't hurt you.

they will ask:

does it hurt?

does it hurt your bones to be so on guard?

are you tense?

are you ever relaxed?

do your muscles ever get to rest?

do spiders crawl inside your skin,

and threaten to tear you apart from within?

you will tell them:

no.

you will tell them:

i am fine. i am fine. i am fine.

but the answer, you know,

is always yes.

yes. it hurts. it hurts. it hurts

PART FOUR: FOR LOVE ITSELF

1.

KALEIDOSCOPE

You are vibrantly coloured,

and they are ever changing.

Within you is a light, warm and bright,

and it illuminates you from within.

A magnificent kaleidoscope of brilliance

all the spectrums hit.

(how to begin —)

Your lips —

a gentleness

I have never known

it is whispering

beckoning to me

I oblige

and it is peace,

like i have never known.

(my breath is caught —)

Your hands —

and tentative touch

reaching for me

trembling softly

afraid to burn

but I am waiting to melt.

Warm me,

hold me,

keep me,

but handle with care.

We are two fragile packages

mishandled far too often.

(— will this last? —)

Your eyes —

full of life

of love

and possibility.

(— and what of my mind? —)

You say,

'Darling, let's not think of tomorrows,

when right now is at our fingertips.'

(— let us pretend —)

I am reflective

of you

in this moment

I am enveloped in your hope.

(— this moment will never end.)

We break

to rebuild together

and for just this moment

a harmony is playing

and the world is singing

a perfect duet.

2.

WINTER

We met just before winter began

but with her it always felt like summer.

I remember because I'm easily cold

and easily miserable.

But when she looked at me and said hello

I felt this burst of colour

as if up to that moment I had been living in greyscale

and I had no idea.

With her I found a love I didn't think was possible

one I hadn't heard of before

one that goes beyond anything I'd ever seen in books or movies.

It wasn't just that she made me complete

it was more that she taught me I was already
whole.

But that didn't mean I couldn't still grow.

We both had our jagged edges

but one by one we stripped them of each
other

like clothes on the bedroom floor.

We were always so easily lost

within our own worlds

we forgot that just because we could no
longer feel it

didn't mean that the world ceased to be cold.

Love heals all.

Love overcomes all.

And though you cannot love

someone's illness away.

Sometimes it is best

to love them at all.

3.

FIRE

I love your flowers,

even when you try and t e a r them at the
roots.

I love your flames,

even when you force   them
out

         —before they can spread.

I love your light,

even when you hide it behind

layers   and

        lay

          er

       s

of stone.

See, what I'm saying is—

I love you

and I will love you

even when you can't love yourself.

4.

KNOWING

I believe the greatest feeling

is simply to be known.

Not necessarily understood

and not quite loved

it's something not to be explained,

only felt.

While at times it is a gift to be unknown

there is something to be said

about the sensation of familiarity

in being plainly seen

through your skin,

behind your teeth,

and deep within your soul;

to be known, purely, as you are.

5.

HONESTY

I once thought

my greatest performance,

was fooling others into believing I'm brave,

that with a stoic face,

I tricked them all,

and carried on

with the world on my shoulders.

The truth is,

I am afraid,

I shake at the slightest of sounds,

and there are days when I fear

walking hallways alone.

To this day,

I am unable to step foot

back into a club,

nor can I wander by a pool

at night on my own.

To this day,

I clench my fists

until my nails break skin

when i am left alone

with a man.

To this day,

my heart pounds in my chest,

as I fear those I love

will one day leave me,

as though nothing I have done

before a mistake matters as much

as the error I had made.

To this day,

I am afraid of my mind,

afraid of one day waking up

and finding I am back

where I had started.

I thought these things

made me a coward,

that because I bore

the fear of the world

pressed against my back,

I was not brave,

but weak

for crumbling against it.

The truth is,

what I must share with anyone

who will listen,

I am still here.

I am still fighting.

I am still opening my heart up

to the universe,

and handing it along

with trembling hands

to those who ask kindly.

And that,

I have learned,

makes one brave.

6.

TEARS

I weep

for the child inside of you,

for the child that was taken,

and placed in a box,

left to survive alone

in the pouring rain.

I weep

for the pain you have suffered,

for the way your heart rests,

torn up and tangled in your chest,

kept together,

with safety pins and duct tape,

precariously balanced.

I weep

for the mistakes you have made,

the ones you carry,

the ones that come out at night,

and whisper that you are not worthy.

I weep

for how the world has taught you

to be afraid,

to tuck away your feelings,

as if they were freshly clean sheets,

and not raw, and real.

I weep

because you believe

you do not matter,

that if all we are

is atoms and dust,

then what could you be,

if not a shallow and empty shell?

I weep

for the fallen,

the broken,

the weary,

and those who believe

they are not allowed

to shatter

to rebuild

and to shatter again.

I weep

because I know not

how to save you,

how to hold you,

how to make you understand

that though this world

is full of cruel,

and evil,

that though we are

but one in seven billion,

you are endlessly

significant

you are created

with a beating heart in your chest,

and tens of millions

of little cells

all working to keep you there

I weep,

because I know what you do not:

that it was not your fault,

—no, truly, it was not—

that you are allowed to rest,

you are allowed to grieve,

and,

above all,

you are allowed to feel.

> — *you are matter, therefore, you
>   matter.*

.

7.

GROWING

I am learning

to not be ashamed

of my illness

I am learning to understand

it is a part of who I am

but it is not all I am.

My scars are littered

across my body.

They are faint now

barely noticeable

no longer a blaring siren

reminding those with prying eyes

that I am all appearances.

But I am no longer ashamed

of the marks I will bear

for the rest of my life

of the tattoos that once read:

'I believe,

if I could create the right

chemical reaction,

if my blood cells,

would react with oxygen,

if I could just

bleed out the sickness,

I would find my solution'

because to me,

now they read:

'I have climbed this hill,

and perhaps

I will fall again,

but I am far beyond

rock bottom now.

See, I have dated death

and decided

he was not

the man for me.'

I am not a victim,

built from glass,

ready to shatter,

but instead

I am a survivor,

forged from steel

no iceberg could sink.

8.

MAMA

My mama told me

she gave me the heart of a wolf,

the voice of a lion

and the skin of a cockroach.

And when I replied with disdain,

she frowned and said,

'Baby, don't you know?

Yes, they are hated and crushed,

but not even a nuclear blast

could tear them down.'

My mama called me buttercup,

pretty and sweet,

but poisonous when threatened.

My mama called me sunflower,

always rising towards the sun

My mama told me I am the dirt, the wind,
and the rain,

no disaster can end the earth

that rests within my skin

She said,

'Baby, you are a star,

burning bright and fierce,

hydrogen and helium burn within your chest,

you are bright light,

and heaven help

the darkness that threatens to claim you,

for you will swallow it whole

and in the end:

you will still shine.'

9.

BRAVERY

I do not like to be called

A very Strong Woman.

I do not like to be told

I am a very Brave Woman.

Though there may be days,

when my strength can match

a thousand suns

when my bravery is that

of twelve hundred lions

when I feel so proud of the skin I am in,

when I feel as though I could take on any king,

these days are not for always.

This strength is fleeting.

Forget strong women.

Forget brave women.

Forget the proud suffering,

forget the muscles borne.

Why is it that we must

either be quiet and weak,

or brave and loud?

Can we not be everything, all at once?

Is it so wrong for a woman to be weak,

to be crippled by her illness,

to be in the dark,

untoward and unclean,

for several weeks at a time?

Do not turn up your nose at these women.

This is what illness is.

This is what this illness does.

It is the woman

who has sobbed openly on the train,

the woman

who has not left her house in three days,

the woman

who has asked you, over and over,

Do you hate me? Do you hate me? Do you
hate me?

This is a ballad for the weak women.

The women who have crumpled

Like leaves in autumn

Crushed beneath the weight

Of their illness,

The type for which there are no words.

This is a ballad for the bad days.

The days when you are bitter, angry, jealous

The days when you are melancholy,
nostalgic, alone

The days not enough poetry is written about.

The days you are ended, ended, ended.

This is a ballad for you, and you, and you.

What is weakness, if not ugly and unseemly?

And what is so wrong with ugly things?

Life is full of all sorts of odds and ends

And perhaps there is no beauty in your illness

But beauty is no cure either way.

Show me your weak women,

your scared women,

your lonely women,

and your trying women.

I am not A Very Strong Woman.

I am not A Very Brave Woman.

Most days I am not a woman at all.

I am, always have, always will be:

Simply put—trying, trying, trying.

10.

SEESAW

I have been living

on a seesaw of emotion,

jumping from addiction to addiction.

Whatever it takes to fill the void.

Anything but the emptiness.

But now,

it occurs to me

—somewhat scandalously, somewhat
provocatively—

there is a chance for both.

There is a chance to live appropriately,

and to live in adventure,

all at once.

To still feel a mountain within me

without losing oxygen in the altitude.

We come from dirt,

we end in dirt,

but the in-between

is left blissfully blank.

All life is—

every year,

every month,

and day, or minute, or hour,

or second and millisecond—

is a beginning.

Begin, begin, begin, begin.

We begin in dirt.

We begin in the parenthesis of the in

between.

We begin in dirt again.

And so the cycle goes,

always turning,

and never once ending.

AFTERWORD

i shut my eyes and close my mind

and open myself up to the possibilities of my
feelings,

see writing for me is not a method of work,

nor is it something i particularly take pride
in,

writing to me is an expression of myself,

an extension of my human experience,

the only way in which i can communicate.

you asked me what it was i spent all my time
writing about

and i found i had no answer,

i found that my writing was just

a stream of consciousness,

sometimes broken apart into numerous lines,

but there was no difference

between

writing

like

this

and writing paragraphs in one sitting.

i share not for the opportunity of exposure,

or money,

however motivating it may be,

but rather because it occurred to me one day,

that while i sat in a dark room and kept my
feelings locked in a suede journal,

that while i suffered in silence and forged

tears into words,

that someone out there may be feeling the
same way,

that someone might be sitting in a dark room,

cold and without a match,

and that somehow,

the match i lit

could make them warm

i told you once that words would get caught
in my throat like knives,

that speaking felt as if i had taken a fork and
shoved it in a toaster,

that my hair stood on end and my skin
prickled at the very idea,

that someone reached in and took my lungs
with both hands

and squeezed

squeezed

squeezed,

that a voice would appear in my mind and
tell me i was not allowed to speak,

to share,

that my feelings were worth no one's time,

that even the worst of souls had more right to
speak than i did.

i can't tell you when i first started writing,

i can't explain when i began to write poetry,

or whatever you'll choose to call this,

i can tell you instead,

that i haven't stopped since.

Printed in Poland
by Amazon Fulfillment
Poland Sp. z o.o., Wrocław